ESTHER

By Rachel Braun • Illustrated by Ma~~~~

For information regarding permission, additional educational resources, and more, visit branchesband.com.
ISBN 978-1-7356228-0-4

Mordecai lived in Babylon
and raised
his orphaned cousin.

Hadassah, known as Esther, too,
was beautiful and was a Jew.

The king desired her for his own.
His royal favor she had won.
He made her queen and crowned her head;

... gave a banquet where all were fed.

Esther and Mordecai, by grace,
were put in place
to save the Jewish race.

Later the king honored Haman.
All should bow when he walks in.

Haman cried,
"This man
should die!"

Getting Mordecai wasn't all:
Haman declared each Jew would fall.
Great was mourning among the Jews;
They weeped and wailed, ate no food.

Esther and Mordecai, by grace,
were put in place to save the Jewish race.
Mordecai told the queen this plan:
"Beg for mercy; save us if you can!"

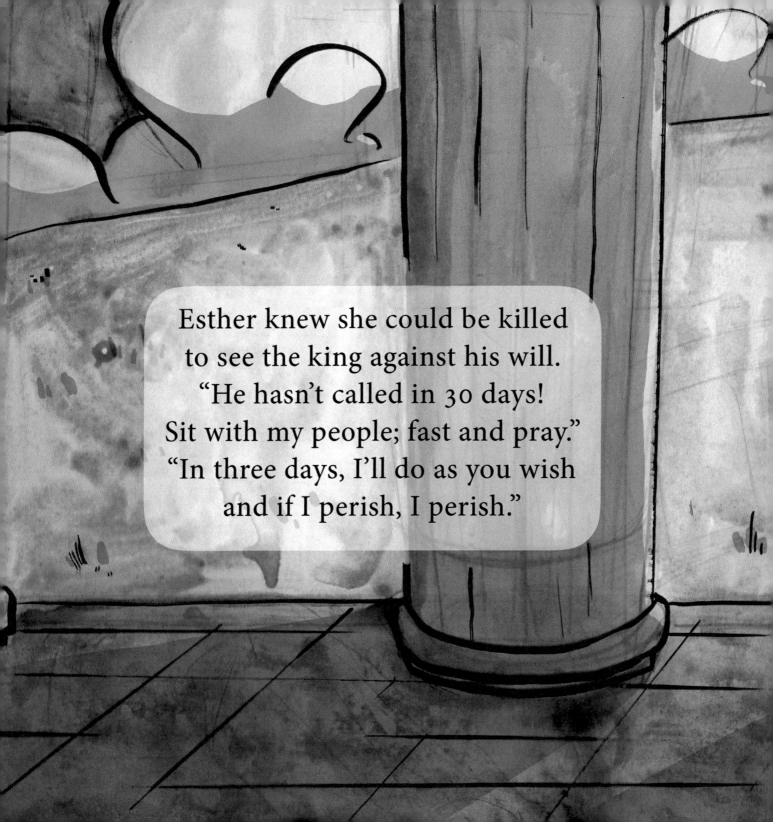

Esther knew she could be killed
to see the king against his will.
"He hasn't called in 30 days!
Sit with my people; fast and pray."
"In three days, I'll do as you wish
and if I perish, I perish."

Esther appeared before the king.
He said, "Ask me for anything!"
She said, "Come eat, bring Haman, too.
I will prepare a meal for you."

The king declared
that he should die

On a pole meant
for Mordecai.

Esther and Mordecai, by grace,
were put in place to save the Jewish race.
A law was passed which gave the right
For every Jew to stand and fight.

The Jews could feast and celebrate!
They were saved from an awful fate.

Esther and Mordecai, by grace,
were put in place
to save the Jewish race.

Haman had an evil plot
He wanted every Jew to rot
Esther went before the king,
Through faith and strength, and as the queen.
Though the king could have her head,
She saved her people from their death.

Esther and Mordecai, by grace,
were put in place to save the Jewish race.

Find the "Esther" song and much more!

Esther started out as a children's song on Branches Band's second children's album: "Grow in the Vine". You can find this album and songbook (as well as many other resources for your home, church, and classroom) at:

branchesband.com

To my Gloria: May God's grace put you where he needs you.

Rachel Braun is a full-time traveling musician and all-the-time mom. She is passionate about reaching children with music and teaching them God's Word. She received her BA in Music, Vocal Performance from Wisconsin Lutheran College. There she met her husband, Andy, and right after graduating, got married and started on this crazy musician adventure. Being a part of Branches Band has allowed her to sing in all 50 states and Canada, as well as write original songs and hymns arrangements. Re-telling the story of Esther, first in an original song, and now through collaboration on this first children's book has been a dream-fulfilling endeavor that will hopefully continue to be replicated!

To my parents: Thank you for filling my childhood with paper and crayons.

Maida Jaspersen is a young creative excited to jump into the world of college. She is a constant creator; whether making a sketchbook, painting portraits of her family, or folding paper airplanes out of placemats, Maida is always on the lookout for a way to produce something for others to enjoy. Esther was a huge blessing, a valuable learning experience, and hopefully the first of many children's books. She will continue to grow her artistic skills at Bethany Lutheran College in Mankato, Minnesota. There she will study Studio Art and load her schedule with as many creative classes as possible.

The text of this book is set in Adobe Hebrew.
The illustrations are in watercolor and ink.